Alphabets and Images

Inspiration from letterforms

Alphabets and Images
Inspiration from letterforms

Maggie Gordon

B T Batsford Limited
London and Sydney

ISBN 0 7134 2878 3

Filmset by Tradespools Limited, Frome, Somerset
Printed by Tinling (1973) Limited, Prescot, Merseyside
(a member of the Oxley Printing Group Ltd.)
for the publisher B T Batsford Limited
4 Fitzhardinge Street, London W1H 0AH and
23 Cross Street, PP Box 586, Brookvale, NSW 2100

Contents

Acknowledgment

I would like to thank my husband for his persistent encouragement, my two children for their lively interest in this book, Gerald Woods and Mrs Elliott and their help, Paul Clark for providing material and the following for supplying illustrations of their work:

David Atkinson

Hilary Beck

Peter Bridgewater

Bronwen Careless

Paul Clark

Andrew Cole

Amy-Louise Gordon

Bob Gordon

Patrick Gordon

Mark Jamieson

Charlotte Knox

Valerie Lawrence

Peter Luff

Jacqui McClennan

Michael McNeil

Sue Morley

Paul Munden

Tony Reid

David Rouse

Alan Skinner

Marilyn Tuck

Gerald Woods

Keith Worthington

Chris Wozencraft

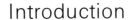

Introduction

In compiling this book I have tried to show just a few of the many interesting and varied ways of looking at letterforms. There are of course many, many more, but the intention of producing such a book is to let it act as a springboard for people with ideas of their own. None of the experiments is intended to be commercially functional in any way; they are simply the result of playing with letterforms in particular contexts. For this reason, wherever possible, I have deliberately avoided showing exercises which require the use of sophisticated equipment. Where this is not possible, I have put forward alternative methods.

I hope that the book will be of help and interest to people directly involved with the use of letterforms as shapes, as well as those using them in a more academic sense. It should encourage children to enjoy the letters they have to learn, memorize, read and write at school, as well as to create in most of us an awareness of the interesting letterforms that exist in our immediate surroundings.

Composition using large and small wooden type to make a simple letter pattern with recognizable shapes

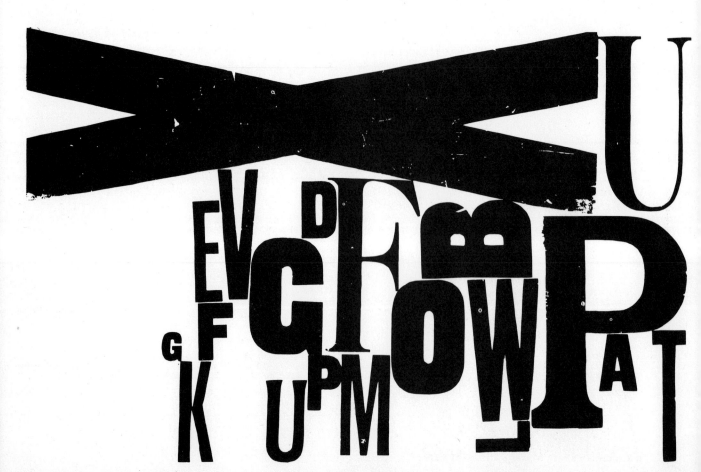

Letters as pattern

Counter shape of the letter A

Children when they first become aware of letters see them as abstract shapes and learn that each shape has its own sound. When these are put together they make a collective sound, a word. They can then associate this new shape with something they know or feel through their senses. Shapes arranged collectively produce more words until they grow into whole pages of books.

Forgetting for the moment the letter's sound, concentrate purely on its abstract shape, looking both at the space surrounding the letter and that inside it; in fact explore letterforms from as many different pattern angles as possible.

For most of the exercises shown in this section only simple equipment is needed:
black and white cartridge paper
scissors
scalpel
Cow gum
printing ink
wooden type letters
(If wooden type is not available, the letters required could be cut from strawboard, [*in reverse*], glued onto a base board, inked up and used in the same way as the type.) These ideas can be interpreted in other media as well, using more sophisticated methods.

Discovering the critical parts of a letter. The student had to decide which parts to retain in order not to lose the visual identity of each letter of the alphabet

opposite Gradual loss of identity. This was achieved by using only the counter shapes of the letters

12

Free play with counter shapes; exploring the
possibilities of portrait and landscape formats

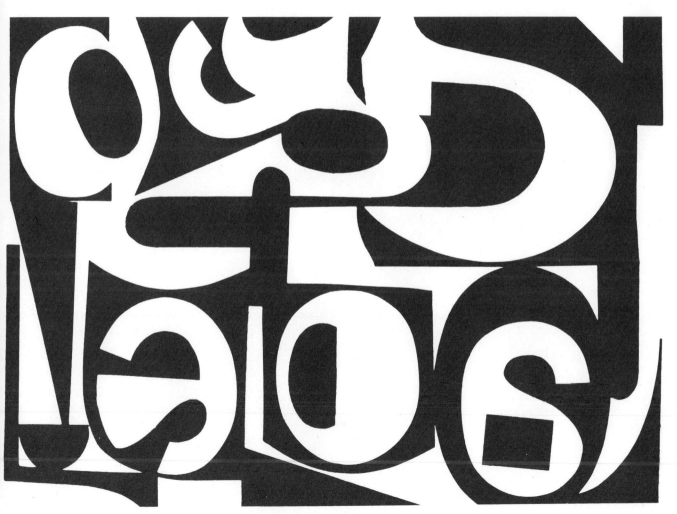

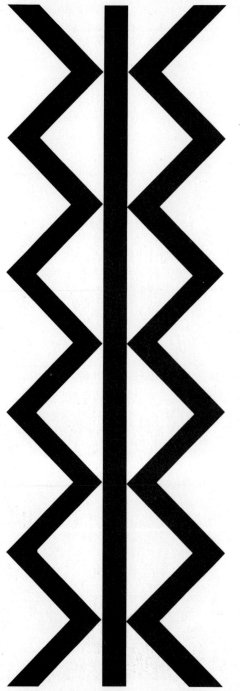

An exercise carried out making use of the
negative form together with contrast in size,
weight, disposition and orientation of the
individual letter forms

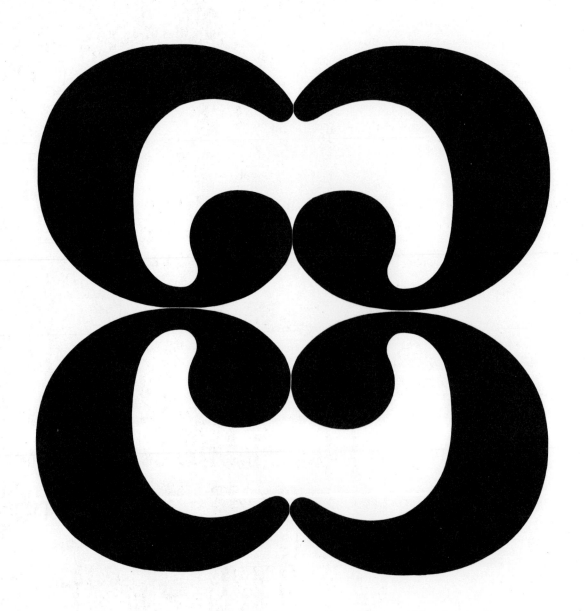

Repetition of the mirrored lower case character c

Combined use of different aspects of letterforms:
form, counter form, positive, negative, size and
weight, all used within a defined area

Looking for letterforms

Every day we look at, even if we do not consciously read, the written word. Driving or walking we see sign posts, instructions painted on the road, advertisements or hoardings besides other things that often go unnoticed: a tremendous variety of letterforms in very different contexts. We accept them as part of our life.

The urge to get away from it all may only be a subconscious realization that these products of our urban civilization are so close to us that we feel put upon. The constant bombardment of visual images and information is simply too much.

However, instead of running away from it all this section does just the opposite: it takes a new look at the purely visual side of our immediate surroundings, indeed even to go so far as to make letter shapes from the objects around us, from our own individual environment.

Collage with letters selected from any printed
material to hand

A collection of various rubbings of letters on buildings and other such objects

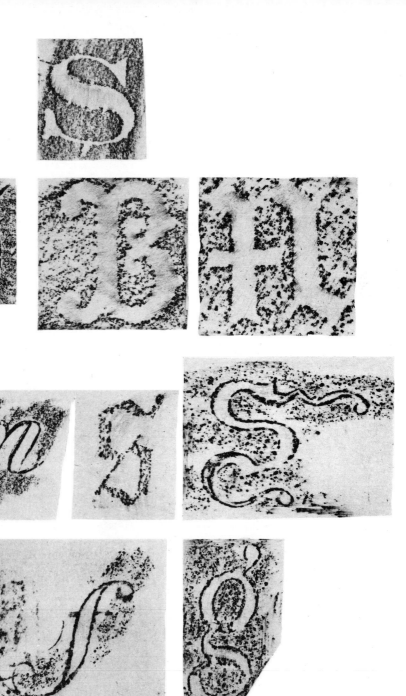

AGED

... GRATEFUL HEART ...
ONE WILL REMEMBER ... THIS

THE LORD ...
BLESSED B ...

ALSO THE ABOVE
THOMAS G...
SOUTH VILLAS
LATE OF KNIGHT...
WHO DIED 27TH OCT
AGED 77 YEARS
FEAR NOT
GOD HAS REDEEMED US
HIS SON OUR SAVIOUR JESUS

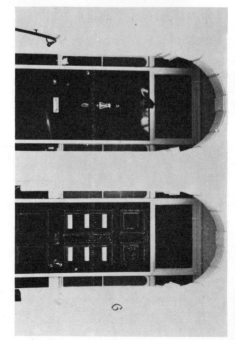

A photographic alphabet
This particular exercise involved, unlike the
previous ones, re-seeing the environment in
such a way that things such as architecture,
traffic lights, park benches and walls were
resolved into letterforms.

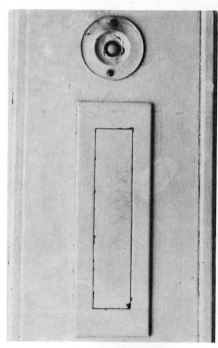

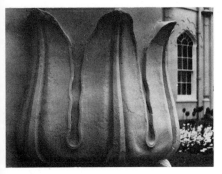

ABCDEFGHIJ
KLMNOPQR
STUVWXYZ
abcdefghijklm
nopqrstuvwxyz

Letters in movement/ Movement within letters

A gradual approach to simple movement with letters arrived at by overprinting and moving the paper vertically

ABCDEFGHIJ
KLMNOPQR
STUVWXYZ
abcdefghijklm
nopqrstuvwxyz

Here are a few of the ways in which movement can be introduced to letterforms both directly and indirectly. Using the characters in pattern form, as opposed to sound symbols, it is possible to create visually various suggestions of movement, eg an action of scattering or throwing, a feeling of speed, the sensation of shifting vertically or horizontally, the feeling of fragmentation or cracking, and the sense of progression or gradual change.

In the following exercises movement is created by using a collection of different or repeated letters, and by a direct movement or change within the letterform itself.

Scattered letters using a spaghetti alphabet

Two examples of slow but free fragmentation of a complete alphabet

A composition of printed letters which have been fragmented in a controlled way using a simple grid

The composition was first arrived at, a grid then superimposed. The student subsequently cut along the grid lines and re-assembled his now 'fragmented' composition using white space to indicate where the cuts were originally made

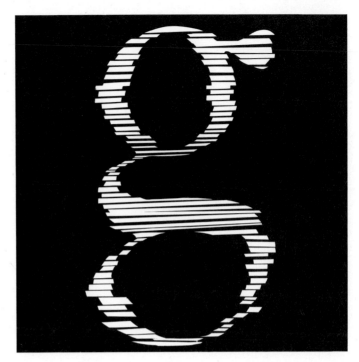

Visual use of horizontal movement within the
letter in order to create a sense of shifting

Slow disintegration of a lower case g

Production of the letter
selected   Disturbance   Disintegration

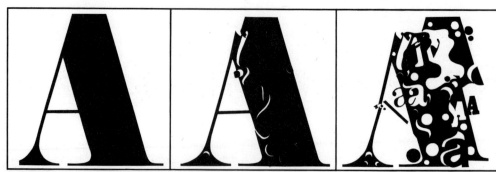

A group experimental exercise

Given seven 200 mm squares of paper, concertina folded, select a letterform. In square 1 draw the character selected, in square 2 create disturbance
3 disintegration
4 diffusion
5 re-collection
6 re-organization
and from this last process, in square 7 evolve a new symbol. First it is necessary to analyse in detail subtle differences between the various processes before attempting to interpret them visually. One of the exciting things about this particular experiment is the complete lack of similarity between any one of the end results, although they were carried out at the same time by a group of students, and the marked visual link between the original character selected and the new symbol.

| Diffusion | Re-collection | Re-organization | Evolution of the new symbol |

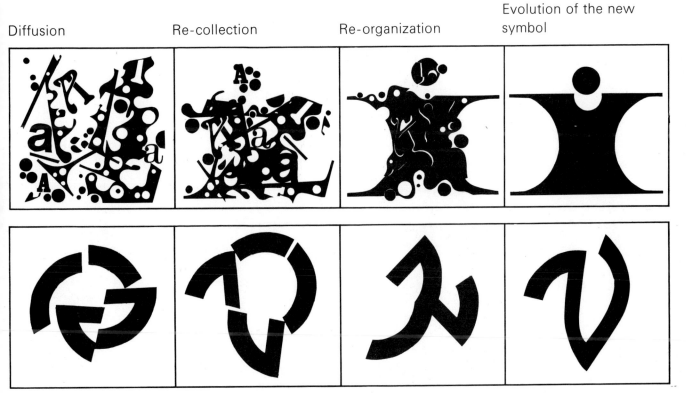

Production of the letter
selected　　　　　　　　Disturbance　　　　　　　Disintegration

Diffusion   Re-collection   Re-organisation   Evolution of the new
symbol

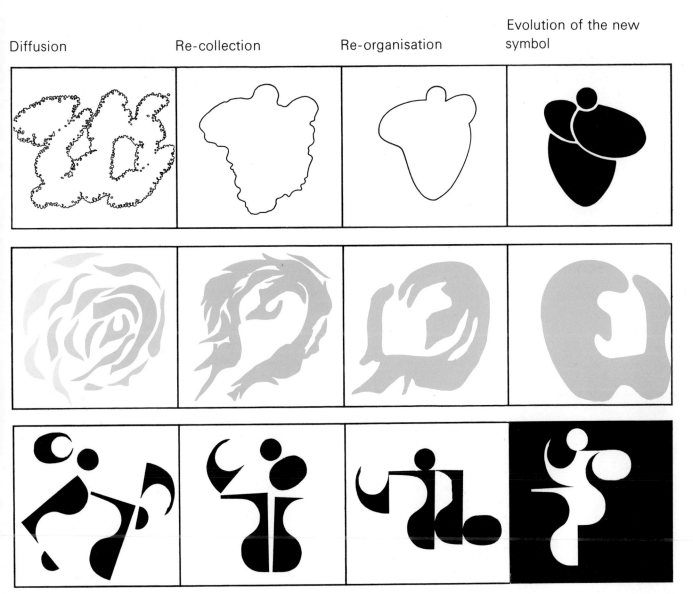

Talking words

Words are a means of communication. When we speak, the listener hears and begins to form his own mental image or sensation of what is being said. When we read, we call upon our imagination to visualize the content matter. Naturally no two readers form exactly the same image.

In this section certain words have been treated in such a way that they have taken on the visual appearance of their meaning. This 'appearance' can be achieved in various ways: by using size, shape, pattern, texture, disposition, space, various methods of printing, colour, doodling, hand lettering and many other techniques. However, before treating words in this way, a thorough understanding of the actual word is needed. So often we think we understand the meaning of a commonplace word, and it is not until such an experiment is undertaken that we fully realize that a much deeper comprehension of the word is needed before we can hope to communicate to others what we ourselves so clearly have in mind.

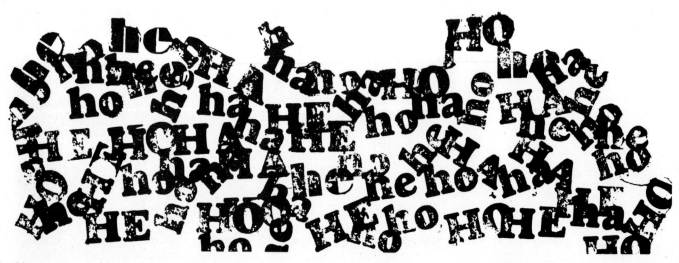

45

spidery

Hi

DREAM

T W E L V E
O
C
L O C K
T

YELLING
YELLING
YELLING
YELLING
YELLING
YELLING
YELLING

a whole heap of YELLING

GLASS

48

rainbow

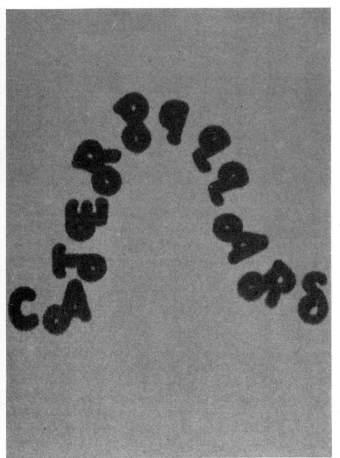

caterpillars

TIN
HUT

string

NEWS

CHEMICAL

BRANDY SNAPS

eclair

Old new

alive ꝺꝺꝺꝺ

WIDE narrow

BIG

SMALL

QUIET loud

SOLID crack

crowd crowd
crowd crowd
crowd crowd
crowd crowd

alone

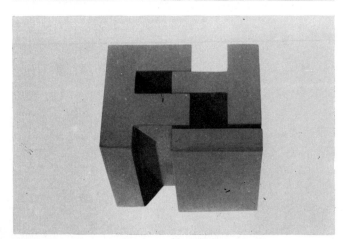

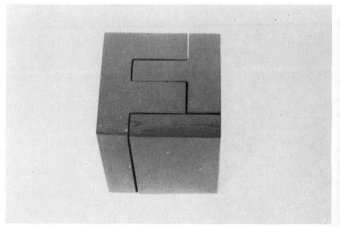

Talking text

When listening to favourite songs, opera or conversations with a particular accent or dialect, it is interesting to visualize in what sort of pattern we would write down the words or how the tonal qualities could be interpreted.

It is easier to carry out such an exercise with a song or accent that has a great personal fascination, one that you feel you understand intimately. When awareness and understanding of free typographic interpretation has developed, it is a challenge to try this with a given text. The two following pages show examples of free personal typographic renderings of typical English and American 'communications'. With the two subsequent illustrations of song interpretation, it is exciting to listen to the music and follow the words of the song as they have been interpreted here.

"Well you know, *it's sort of,* I mean, *well* you know, it's SORT OF, YOU KNOW, I MEAN, well sort of, *you know, it's well sort of.....* [*I agree!*]

Old Ebenezer thought he was JULIUS CÆSAR

they put him in

and so a h o ome

where

they

gave him

Medicinal Compound STRICKLAND & HOLT LTD. DISPENSING CHEMISTS YARM. SHAKE THE BOTTLE

emperor of

he's

and now ROME

56

HEY JUDE don't make it BAD

take a Sad song —

and make it BET———TER

REMEMBER TO LET HER IN-TO YOUR HEART

THEN YOU CAN START

to make it———————BETTER———————

AND ANY-TIME YOU FEEL THE PAIN

HEY JUDE   refrain

don't CAR———RY THE WORLD

UPON YOUR SHOUL-DERS

FOR WELL YOU KNOW THAT IT'S A FOOOL

Who plays   it   COOL

By mak - ing his WORLD

a lit-tle cold-er ———

da   da   da   da   da   da   da

is not for apple

Emotive letters

is for apple

We are so used to taking for granted the sound symbol aspect of letterforms that the emotive content is often missed.

The illustration on the facing page is typical of many seen in children's educational books. We readily accept that this is an A just like any other A, only in this particular case it is identified with 'Apple'. The shape of this A has little visual regard for the object chosen: an apple, which is round in shape, physically tangible, crisp and refreshing in taste. Were this A representing the word 'Angle' it would convey the geometric qualities extremely well visually. The lower case conveys a great deal more 'apple feel'.

There are many ways of exploring this particular aspect of the letterform. To start with the subject matter should be kept simple in order to have a more direct visual appeal in the end result. However, as we become more aware and sensitive to letterforms, and are prepared to spend time researching into the feel and meaning of the subject matter, a complete personal alphabet, along the lines of that shown on pages 64 to 71 could be devised.

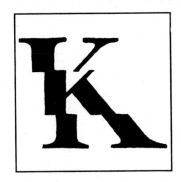

killing

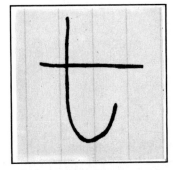

teaching

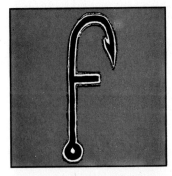

fishing

Queen

A great greedy G

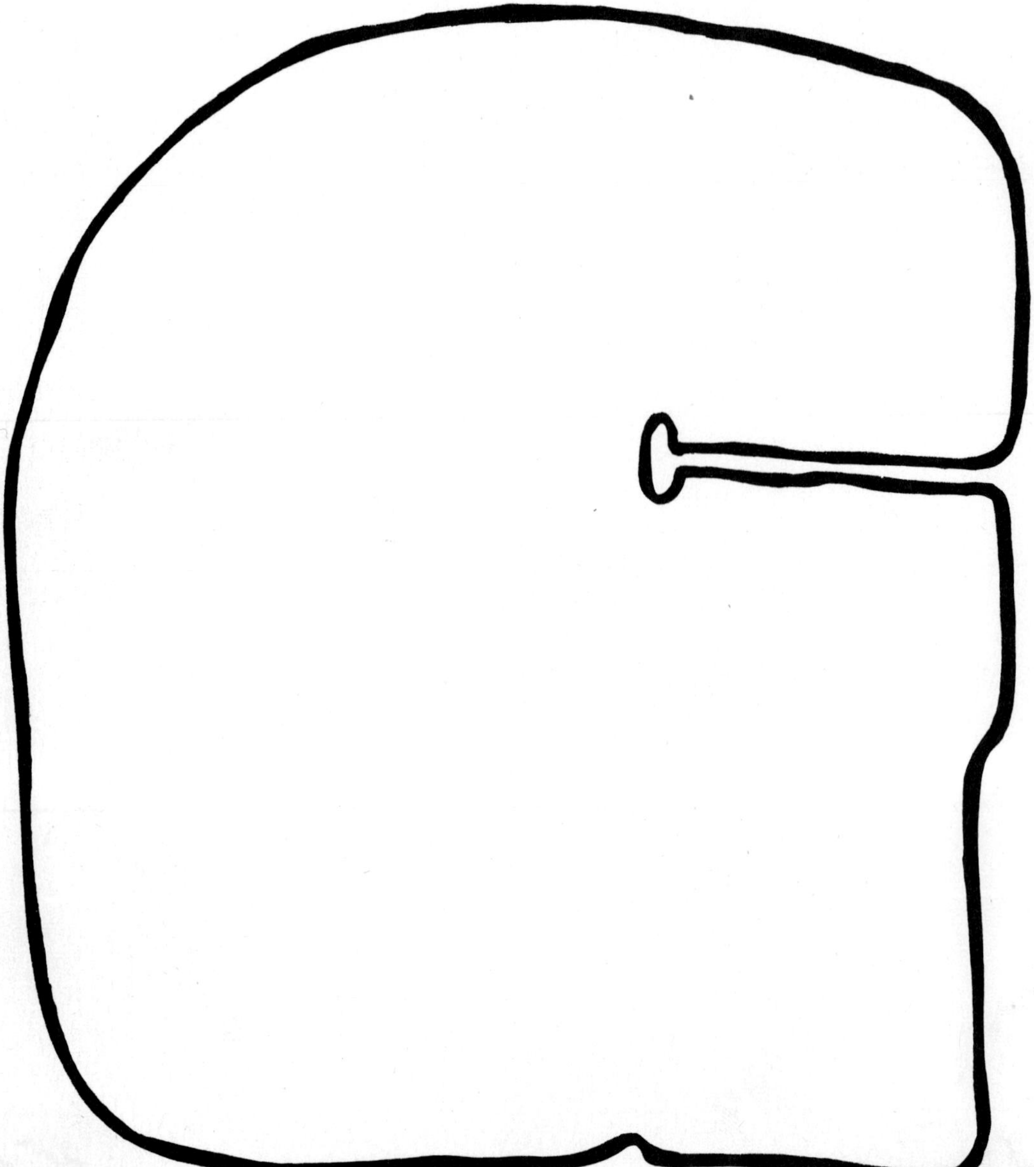

A mean miserable M

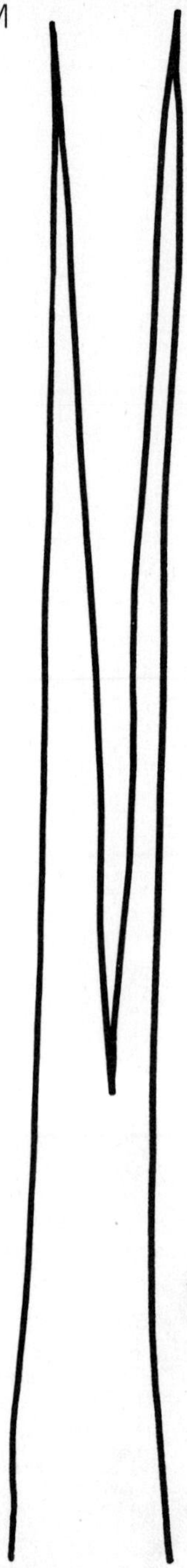

Electric E

An adults' alphabet

boredom

B B B B B B B
B B B B
B B B
B B
B
B
B

contentment

depreciation

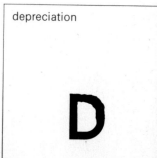

fantasy

generation

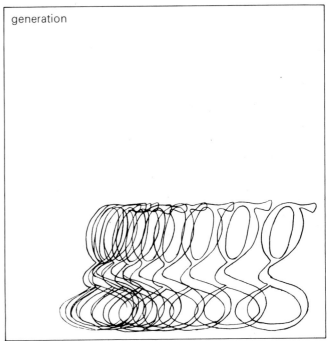

elation

hesitation

introvertion

jubilation

kaleidoscopic

lavishness

memory

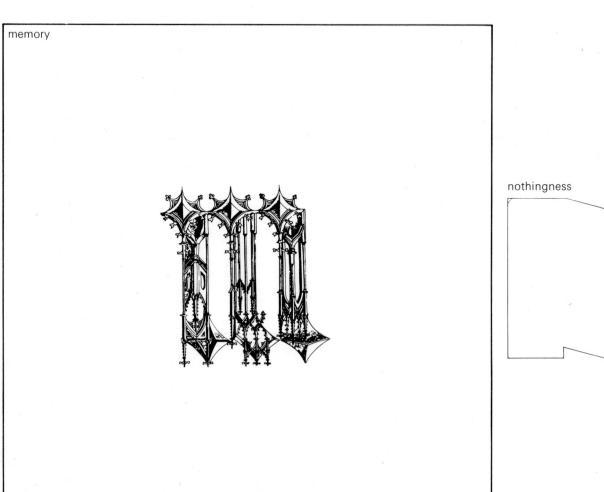

nothingness

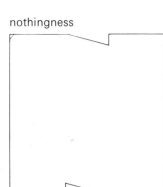

oblivion

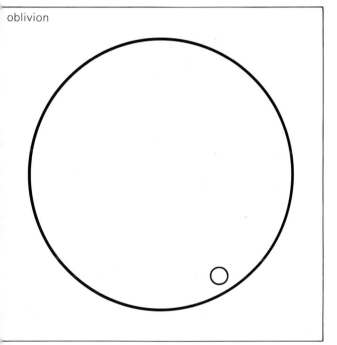

purification

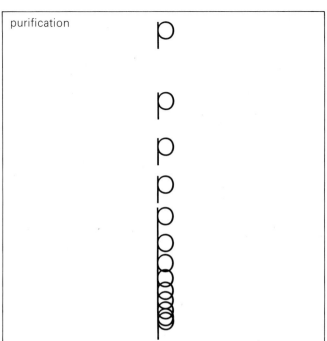

queerness

retrospection

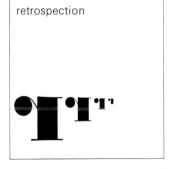

schizophrenic

unconsciousness

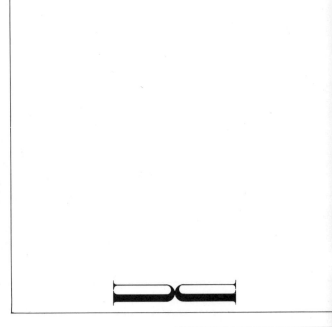

terrorization

verbosity

wantonness

xylographic

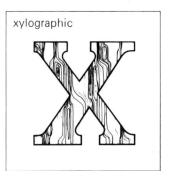

ypsilonform

zealousness

71

```
       "Fury said to
          a mouse, That
             he met in the
                house, 'Let
                   us both go
                      to law: I
                         will prose-
                            cute you.
                         Come, I'll
                      take no de-
                   nial; We
                must have
             a trial:
          For really
       this morn-
    ing I've
 nothing
 to do.'
       Said the
          mouse to
             the cur,
                'Such a
                   trial, dear
                      Sir, With
                         no jury
                            or judge,
                               w o u l d
                                  be wast-
                                     ing our
                                        breath.'
                            'I'll be
                         judge,
                      I'll be
                   jury,'
                Said
             cun-
             ning
                old
                   Fury:
                      'I'll
                         t r y
                            the
                               whole
                                  cause,
                                     a n d
                                        con-
                                           demn
                                          you to
                                       death.'"
```

Mass and texture

In this context, *mass* is defined as a collection of printed matter: in newspapers, magazines and books, as well as any collection of writing: exercise books, letters and shopping lists; and *texture* as the visual feel of the surface presented by this mass. Being concerned with the actual content of 'mass', we tend to miss the visual textural quality. In this section the emphasis is placed on the exciting visual effect. Exploration into mass can be taken a stage further by relating the total content to the finished visual effect as so clearly indicated by the example on the left.

Simple handwriting when used as the only material for a collage gives a lively, uneven visual texture.

man out of peices. I
and is Just what he
rain in aswell. one night
some lightning struck Just
Frankenstien was
When it stopped
to the ground. professer
ever wanted to make a
other side of the world
name was professer
cula" so he did. But
make two twins I said

re-join pattern if necessary. through
industrial hotel work Quit morning
(one outside) total work
facing and fabric.
to collapsed peices of
against wrong.
paper are
fabric layer
of fabric

Viking cage-men
1000 and AD 105 sh deep
hilde Fjord mere interestg day
of barriers to put all new in
town of Roof capital of Georgia
The five Viking
are

THEA
cot ij
the ol

This
red.
Clopin
Sally
oberg
North
7:20

Shepherd, shepherd, count your
can't come now I'm fast asle
If you don't come now they wil
Shepherd, come along,
the origin of baseball
lion greater than there is
in North America but she
depart from being nothing
New York and a sloo
than place in a
Green a good

Nikolayevich Kisanov had never been and could
but his heart sank when the
card. They should ha
children to some k

On top of it am
tions ye

my consount
Having a good
apart from a
windscreen, var
t mosquito

Senn + yu

r wing was number thi

WUSd
old
s. Hey
s Daddy ist-here
you will be doing
his job inste Frankenstien
I wonder She will ma
will be Frankenstie I will
I didenj ard Just then
he came all
professer Frankens

upo tin tha
woh An and
m An and
livd In a
wu nAy

Once I built a
A great tall on
I built it out of
I dressed him in
And I called hi

Nikolayevich Kisanov
Frankenstien put a

in Moscow here
(where Gagarin
before

We also
capitals of
like 3 very interest
looking and 3 ir
Albanian Tirani
Moscow Tbilisi

When we look at unfamiliar alphabets, our eyes are forced to view initially the purely textural quality.

A more exacting exercise is to divide a given area into equal squares and fill these with varied textures of printed matter in order to create a sense of planes lying flat, projecting and receding.

Russian

Идя навстречу требованиям жизни и по желаниям наших читателей, мы изменяем ся, расширяемся и совершенствуемся.

Стремясь решить труднейшую задачу удовлетворения запросов самых разно образных категорий читателей, мы осве щаем широкий круг вопросов: печатное дело, оформление, история, археология философия, поэзия и даже незатейливые приключенческие рассказы из жизни джунглей. Когда мы оглядываемся назад то мы ищем вдохновения для будущего. Когда мы глядим вперед, то мы надеемся помочь кампании за модернизацию печат

Arabic

لقد توسعنا وتغيرنا ونأمل أن نكون تحسنا. في عام
تغير الأذواق واجهنا مشكلة لم تكن معروفه لسلفنا
وهي محاولة إرضاء إن لم يكن إدخـال الـسـرور على
طبقات كثيرة من القراء في شي الموضوعات:
فلسـفـة وتاريخ، فكاهة وغموض، شعر، تصميم
وطباعة. ونـ نهمل تطليق العلم والمسرح في عصرنا هذا.
ولقد استوحينا من ما فيناالحـاضرنا. وعند ما
نظر الى هـذا المستقبل نؤون بهذا التصنيع القادم،
والمساهمون معنـا رغم إختلافهم سيكونـون صورة
مصغرة لعالم عديد الجنسيات يمثل هدفنا.
أننا نود أن نتحدث مع قرائنا كل بلغته ومقالا
يقدم بأكبر عدد من اللغات على قدر ما يـمـح بـ
المكان وإنا لنعتذر عما يترك رغم إرادتنا.

Hindi

Greek

'Ετροποποιήσαμεν, ἐπεξετείναμεν καί ἐβελ
τιώσαμεν τάς ἐκδόσεις μας ὥστε νά ἀντα
ποκρίνονται πρός τάς ἀξιώσεις τῆς ἐποχῆ
μας καί τάς προσδοκίας τῶν ἀναγνωστῶν μας
Πρός Ικανοποίησιν τῆς μεγάλης ποικιλίας τῶν
ἀναγνωστῶν μας, περιελάβομεν εἰς τάς ἐκδό
σεις μας μίαν εὐρείαν ποικιλίαν θεμάτων:
τυπογραφίαν, σχεδίασμα, Ιστορίαν, ἀρχαιο
λογίαν, φιλοσοφίαν, ποίησιν, ἀκόμη δέ καί
ἀστυνομικά μυθιστορήματα δαιδαλώδους
πλοκῆς. Στρέφοντες τά βλέμματά μας εἰς τό
παρελθόν ἀναζητοῦμεν ἐμπνεύσεις διά τό μέλ
λον. Προσβλέποντες δέ εἰς τό μέλλον ἐλπίζομεν
ὅτι συμβάλλομεν εἰς τό γενικόν αἴτημα διά μίαν

74

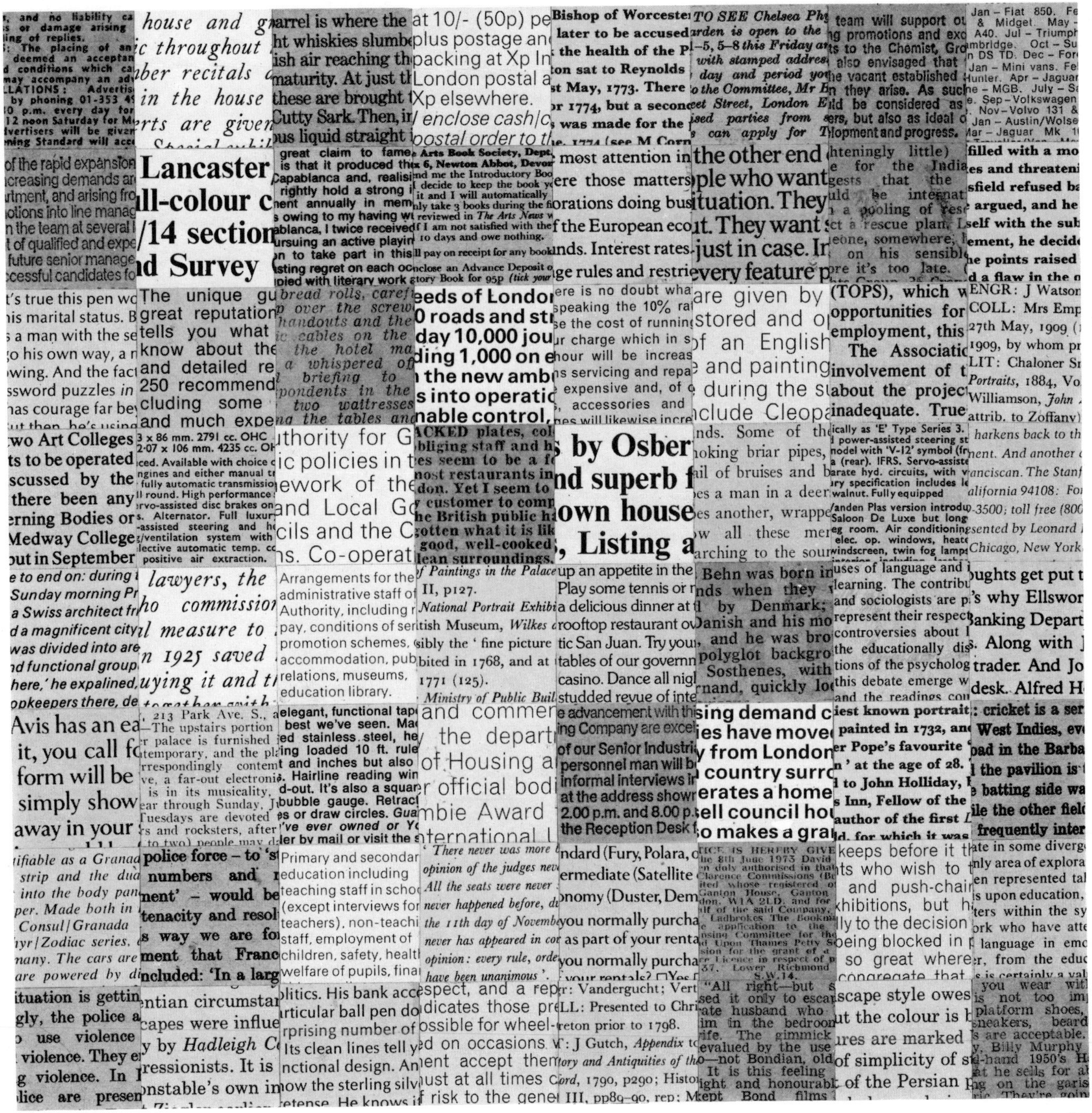

As well as using the organised nature of the typewriter to make rigidly controlled letterforms, by freeing the 'paper grip' unexpected results occur.

safeguard the existing flood defences along the ba
hours or perhaps as late as four hours before high
trigger the start of a countdown for barrier closur
misery and suffering. The moral is obvious – it jus1
also minimises interference with amenity. The diac
been done to give more protection where the risk i
height. In fact some emergency wall raising has alı
the warning would either be cancelled or confirmɛ
greatest. Most of these temporary defences could
cost and speed of construction over the other typ
without taking into account the cost of life, sheeı
If very abnormal weather conditions coincide witl
used to bring the barrier into action. This provide:
could paralyse the central part of the undergroun
to the problem it offers tremendous advantages in
government buildings. No one can assess the prol
and could knock out power, gas and water suppli
thousands of homes, shops, factories, businesses
telephone and teleprinter services and severely hi
tide there would be a flood disaster in London wh
give the usual advance warning to shipping. Poss

the operating machinery until in the fully raised p

the sector gates are swung up out of their housin

sight in their housings on the river bed. In an eme

average high tides at London Bridge are currently

requirements – and when not in use the gates are

show the construction of the barrier. The four mɛ

Because the Thames could turn into a killer overn

general tides are rising. The combined effect is su

design is already going ahead and will take about

Looking at actual lines of type, we can
see where white space has been allowed to play
a part in the completed experiment. This has
been achieved in both random and controlled
ways.

TYPOGRAPHIC

TYPOGRAPHICTYPOGRAPHICTYPOGRAPHICTYPOGRAPHIC

TYPOGRAPHICTYPOGRAPHICTYPOGRAPHICTYPOGRAPHIC

TYPOGRAPHICTYPOGRAPHICTYPOGRAPHICTYPOGRAPHIC

TYPOGRAPHICTYPOGRAPHICTYPOGRAPHICTYPOGRAPHIC

ness of fit. In a serifed – especially a slab-serife
eness of fit can present problems : there is a tend
unserifed, rounded characters to appear loose. In
ockwell, this fault has been largely avoided.
cent serifs all but touch, such characters as b, c, d,
q do not spoil the even flow of the line. This is due
extra width and height of the rounded parts of thes
h allow them amply to fill their respective position
ying attention to the inter-character space. It is po
cise individual combinations of letters – no type de
erfect on this score – but the overall appearance
ers, and in this respect Rockwell is particularly suc
hat purpose then can Rockwell serve us today?
of the excessive use of sanserifs in jobbing work
ed face of the style of Rockwell can offer a pleasing
It may be less readable – always a difficult point to
rove – and one cannot visualise its being suitable
ngs, but it remains a clear, closely-fitting, well-in
Its family is nicely balanced, and its monoline ch
lend themselves to photomechanical reproducti

il the even flow of the line
nd height of the rounded
n amply to fill their respe
n to the inter-character s
al combinations of letters
is score – but the overa
his respect Rockwell is pa
then can Rockwell serv
ssive use of sanserifs in
e style of Rockwell can of

er-character
tions of letter
but the over
Rockwell is p
Rockwell ser

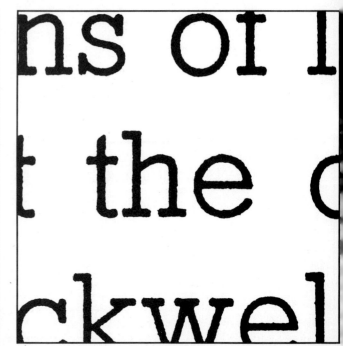

ns of l
t the c
ckwel

Radically enlarging a defined area of type allows the reader to become aware of the size and texture of the mass content.

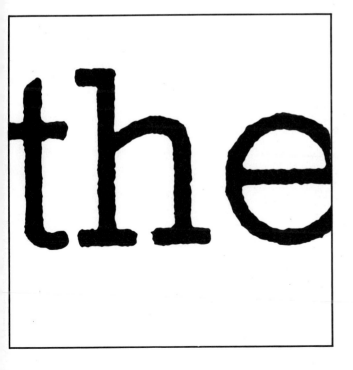

At the end of the war London faced an acute housing shortage. No new building had taken place for six years and many people had lost bombing: couples married younger during the wartime and wanted to set up home on their own. The LCC had put (prefabs) on vac
but it was always intended that these would y a temporary palliative for the crisis. Un-fortunately, these temporary homes used up many up emergency factory made houses of the vacant sites
Council began to look beyond the city's boundaries for space to build its per
held what were for a County
to build houses both inside an,
boundaries but it also faced a rehousing problem ant sites and on the edges of

that was unique in its size—hundreds of thousands their homes of people needed new homes. Over the next few years a number of large low-density estates' were built outside the while the redevelopment progr London was getting under way, until, by 1960 in the nearly 100,000 people had mo war houses. Harold Hill and Aveley are but tw examples. During this time the Gover introducing legislation to help cope with the crisis.

Under the New Towns Act, 1946 eight new towns, each with an estimated population of 25,000 or more within the London area a were designated to meet the needs of Greater London. nd the In 1952 this ment Act to encourage and of existing towns by agreement between local parks, authorities. By 1962 the LCC had signed sixteen outside town expansion agreeme thirty and sixty miles from London. Eventually amme in inner these sixteen enlarged towns would house 50,000 nts for towns bet ex-London families. However, realising that these old established towns

thrust upon them and that the pace of develop would be relatively slow, the LCC in the mid-fifties asked the Government for permission to ment prepare a scheme in parallel a new town of 100,000 people with

and Local Government began to urge the release of government and railway surplus lands as part of the ween drive to solve the London housing problem. This with these solutions for initiative identified and mapped out a ring of practi-manent houses. cally empty sites, which could be released to re-was reinforced by the T house people, area by area, boroughs so that works of redevelopment could from the crowded inner proceed there. The sites included Hendon and Council unique power Croydon aerodromes, Kidbrooke depot and the

jazz rhythm swing melody tempo beat tune blues pop mood rave
jazz rhythm swing melody tempo beat tune blues pop mood rave
jazz rhythm swing melody tempo beat tune blues pop mood rave
jazz rhythm swing melody tempo beat tune blues pop mood rave
jazz rhythm swing melody tempo beat tune blues pop mood rave
jazz rhythm swing melody tempo beat tune blues pop mood rave
jazz rhythm swing melody tempo beat tune blues pop mood rave
jazz rhythm swing melody tempo beat tune blues pop mood rave
jazz rhythm swing melody tempo beat tune blues pop mood rave
jazz rhythm swing melody tempo beat tune blues pop mood rave
jazz rhythm swing melody tempo beat tune blues pop mood rave
jazz rhythm swing melody tempo beat tune blues pop mood rave
jazz rhythm swing melody tempo beat tune blues pop mood rave
jazz rhythm swing melody tempo beat tune blues pop mood rave
jazz rhythm swing melody tempo beat tune blues pop mood rave
jazz rhythm swing melody tempo beat tune blues pop mood rave
jazz rhythm swing melody tempo beat tune blues pop mood rave
jazz rhythm swing melody tempo beat tune blues pop mood rave
jazz rhythm swing melody tempo beat tune blues pop mood rave
jazz rhythm swing melody tempo
jazz rhythm swing melody

Atmospheric conditions such as sun radiation, fog and rain can be emulated by using various printed or typed letters.

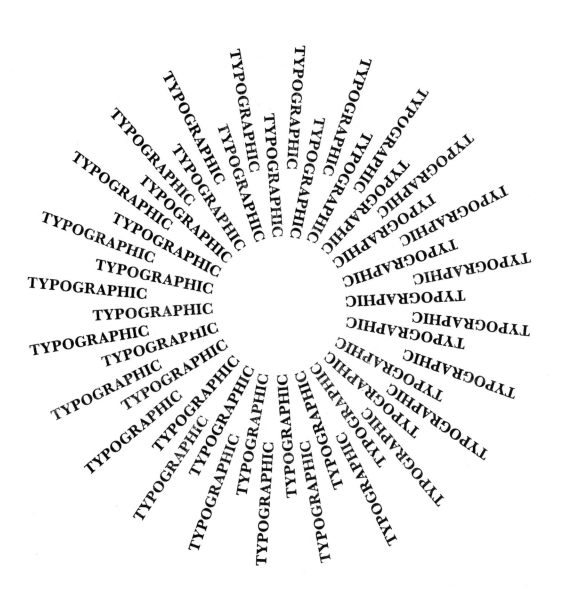

A man-hole cover is interpreted here in hand
drawn 'i's

An abstract pattern made from cash register
bills giving an interesting tonal quality

A symbolic forest created by using a rubber date
stamp

3 4 MAY 1974
3 4 MAY 1974
3 4 MAY 1974
3 4 MAY 1974
3 4 MAY 1974
3 4 MAY 1974
3 4 MAY 1974
3 4 MAY 1974
3 4 MAY 1974
3 4 MAY 1974
3 4 MAY 1974
3 4 MAY 1974
3 4 MAY 1974
3 4 MAY 1974
3 4 MAY 1974
3 4 MAY 1974
3 4 MAY 1974
3 4 MAY 1974
3 4 MAY 1974
3 4 MAY 1974
3 4 MAY 1974
3 4 MAY 1974
3 4 MAY 1974
3 4 MAY 1974
3 4 MAY 1974
3 4 MAY 1974
3 4 MAY 1974
3 4 MAY 1974
3 4 MAY 1974
3 4 MAY 1974
3 4 MAY 1974
3 4 MAY 1974
3 4 MAY 1974
3 4 MAY 1974
3 4 MAY 1974
3 4 MAY 1974
3 4 MAY 1974
3 4 MAY 1974
3 4 MAY 1974
3 4 MAY 1974
3 4 MAY 1974
3 4 MAY 1974
3 4 MAY 1974
3 4 MAY 1974
3 4 MAY 1974
3 4 MAY 1974
3 4 MAY 1974
3 4 MAY 1974

A typographic rendering of a piece of hand-woven
herring-bone tweed has the same visual 'feel'
as the cloth itself

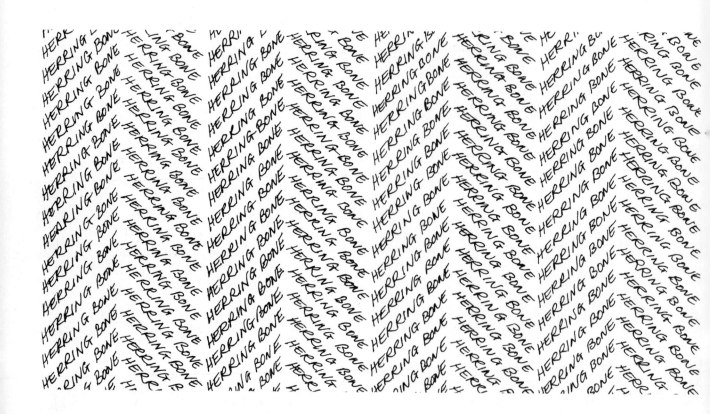

The quality of wrought iron work is evoked through the abstract arrangement of suitable letterforms

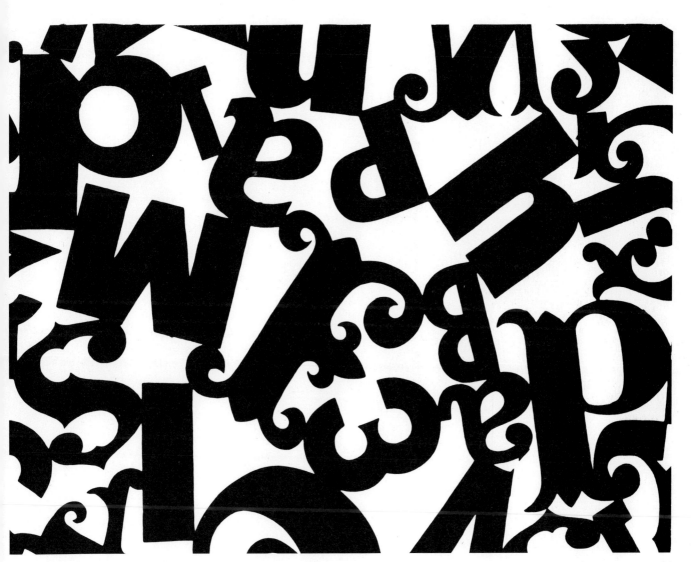

A typographic sea created by using wooden type, hand inking it, and printing it manually in the most evocative position

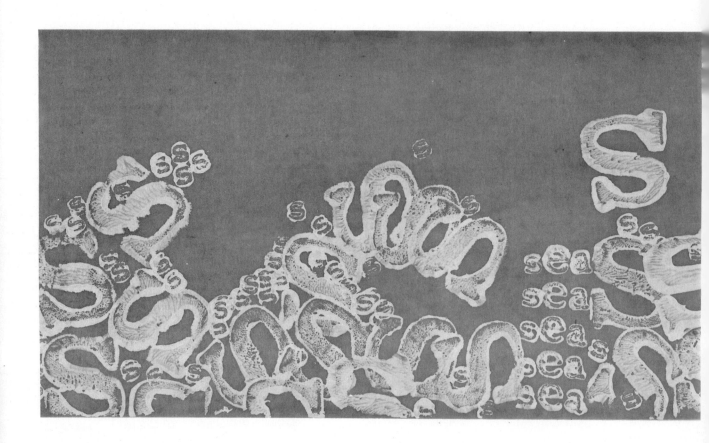

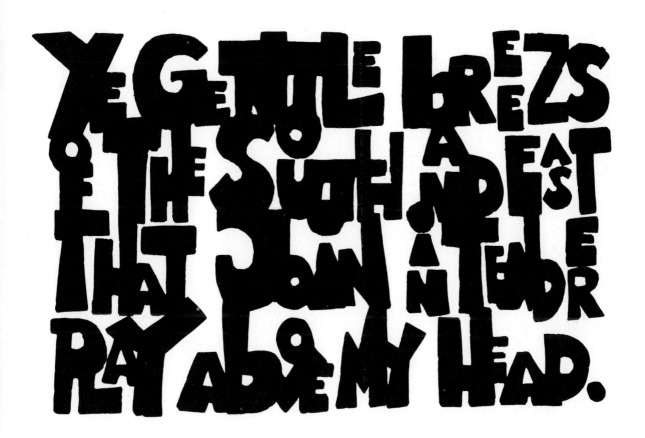

Bright clean blue sky

Pure white smokey trailing clouds

dusting

Ragged grassy hill
covered in dusty purple
cross-stitch patches

thin acid slither of sharp green

musky
petrified
trees

dusty green
mound

Materials

Basic equipment
Scissors
Craft knife or razor blades
Straight edge
Pair of compasses
Set square
Mapping pen
Lettering pen
Pen nibs including italic ones
Instant lettering
Black and white cartridge papers
Tracing paper
Adhesives
Washable lettering ink
Indian ink
Coloured inks
White ink
Assorted colours of gouache or poster paints,
including black and white
Selection of sable hair brushes

Additional useful materials
Instant lettering catalogues
Lino for lino cuts and cutting tools
Potatoes for potato cuts
Any rubber stamps
Inking pad
Ink roller *gelatine*
Tissue paper *a range of colours*
Gummed paper *a range of colours*
Coloured cartridge papers
Stencil kit

Coloured fibre-tip pens
Dictionary
Type specimen book
Camera
Note book
Scrap book for visual notes
Wax crayons for rubbings
Graph paper
Blotting paper
Coloured film for overlaying
Typewriter

Possible sources of finding material
Newspapers
Magazines
Comic books
Labels
Posters
Exercise books
Tickets
Programmes

Adhesives
Cow Gum (rubber cement)   Good for all
lightweight papers
Easy to remove with lighter fuel
Spray adhesive   Very good for sticking large
areas of tissue paper
PVA   Sticks things edge to edge very well
Copydex   Suitable for most things especially
fabrics and collage. Can be removed with amyl
acetate
Polycell (wallpaper paste)   Useful for collage
work as it dries clear
Balsa cement   Good for 3D work.
NB   Impact adhesives are not suitable for
paper work.

Suppliers

Most of the items mentioned are available at any good art store and large stationers or from the following specialists:

Artists materials and equipment

E J Arnold Limited
School Suppliers
Butterley Street
Leeds LS10 1AX

Reeves and Sons Limited
Lincoln Road
Enfield, Middlesex

Winsor and Newton Limited
Wealdstone
Harrow, Middlesex

Papers

G F Kettle
127 High Holborn
London W1

Paperchase Limited
216 Tottenham Court Road
London W1

Instant lettering

Letraset Shop
44 Gerard Street
London W1
A comprehensive catalogue available